THE MANGO TREE

"SEASONS CHANGE"

Deborah Lorde

Published by: Rehoboth Publications

Barbados

THE MANGO TREE

Lorde, Deborah

THE MANGO TREE

ISBN-13: 9798357942890

Printed in the United States of America

TABLE OF CONTENTS

Healing for Fractured Relationships *(Relationship Coaching)*

To Whom It May Concern:

With all the turmoil you are experiencing in your relationship, I know that you believe that things will never change between you and your partner. You may also believe that your partner will never change and things will never get any better. But life around you changes, so why shouldn't you. It may seem as if there is no hope nor any point in continuing along this path but before you give up - here is a thought – change is coming.

Let me encourage you to learn from the season which you are in. The season is here to give you something which you will require for your next season. Store up the good from each season – the abundance which comes with each one - to take you along on your journey. If you are vigilant to notice this abundance, you can store it so that you will have what you need for the next season.

To everything there is a season – there is a time for everything under the sun. In nature a season has a beginning and an end and in relationships this is also true. Know that this too shall pass and the next season will come along with its own blessings and challenges so prepare for each season by opening your heart to what is happening presently.

You grow your faith muscle through perseverance and the next season of your relationship could very well be your best one yet. Even with a simple change in your perspective (thinking), things could significantly improve and get better.

Grow through your seasons.

Introduction:

Watching the Mango tree in my backyard has kept, in the forefront of my mind, the fact that seasons change. Change is the only constant in life and while some of us do not welcome change – most can attest to the fact that it is good that things do not remain the same forever.

The fruit of the mango tree can be very sweet – for the individual with diabetes, some care must be taken on the quantity consumed, but for the rest of us – ummm. The mango is not available all year round because it is subject to its own season.

Look at the cycle that is created – when you love mangoes, you still must endure dead branches, just leaves, blossoms, and then the fruit and the cycle starts all over again. If there are lessons to be learnt, let us consider what the mango tree can teach us.

Chapter One

Your First Season – No Fruit only leaves

You can come to a Mango Tree in any season of its life and where you are is where you start. The seasons will happen regardless of which season you find your tree and these seasons will change without any effort from you.

So, we understand that seasons change. The real test is how do you respond to changes in each season. Are you going to anxiously await the change to the next season, or do you prefer one season over the other? Will you recognize the value in the season or will you fret and bemoan the present season, knowing full well that there is nothing you can do to make it happen any faster than it already does.

We find our Mango Tree at the stage where the tree is full of leaves. All you can see is an abundance of leaves – many of which are in full life and are resistant to the winds because they are young and strong. There is no sight of the fruit itself – but this is a Mango Tree – there is no doubt about that.

Currently, the leaves provide shade so you can sit under the tree, especially to get away from the heat of the day and it is safe since there is no threat of being hit in the head by a falling mango. Some of the leaves fall off and what is required is a major clean-up of the area under that tree, sometimes as a daily chore or it may even need to be done twice a day. Look out!!!!! clean up today and tomorrow you can be assured that more leaves will be there.

What do you do when all you get from the Mango Tree are leaves? Leaves that you must clean up with no reward- not one fruit. This season seems to go on forever and every day you get to work on a mess that you did not create. Is it worth it to carry on with this Mango Tree or should you cut it down in disgust because of all the leaves it sheds causing this unsightly mess.

Hardly would you get rid of your Mango Tree, not if you know that Mangoes are coming. This season will **not** go on forever so go ahead and clean up those fallen leaves under the tree. As you do so, here is your reward – exercise, fresh air, the creation of a haven under the tree, and any other positives which you can determine.

When we focus on the positives, we recognize how the tree, in and of itself, is already a blessing so while we wait on the *Fruit* the current situation is not *all* bad. Persevere, because once we keep going, the rains will eventually start and the season will change.

Lesson 1 – Perseverance without Evidence

What we want to see is Fruit; not only see but taste and enjoy the delicacy of the mango. Can you accept that the tree is a fruit-bearing tree – so eventually mangoes must appear.

Our faith requires us to trust the process, understanding that eventually our patience will be rewarded by fruit. While we wait, we can enjoy the work-out to remain fit in our minds and in our bodies, develop our muscle and get much needed fresh air. The promise remains that while there is currently no evidence that the tree bears fruit, this will soon change if you have the patience to not give up at this stage in the journey.

In life, this season can be troublesome for us to comprehend and hold out the hope we need to carry us through, until the next stage. The work required at this youthful stage of life becomes difficult to endure, sometimes we do not even recognize that our muscles are being developed as we clean up the mess the fallen leaves make. The tree holds so much promise yet there is no evidence of produce – no productivity. Can you get angry with the tree for not being able to bear its fruit?

In our relationships this is the season - early in the process and sometimes because we are in a hurry to move along, we scarcely notice that this process is needed. It is not only necessary for the tree to mature, but also for you to mature as well in your outlook and perspective on life and to learn what is required as you move into the next season.

The journey requires that you look at this tree and see with the eyes of faith that you are going to eventually be able to pick mangoes and enjoy the fruit. You will not pick a few but so many that your abundance may very well overwhelm you. So, wait and while you wait enjoy this stage of the journey until the season changes.

Recognize too that it is not just about waiting for the season to change but also about learning through the process. What lessons are need in this season of your relationship journey.

You may be young or the relationship is at an early stage. You are now learning what is required to make a relationship work. The sacrifice of now having to think of another person and having to put their needs above yours. A level of maturity is required and a shift in mindset that you are now building as you wait and grow and understand who you are becoming.

A lesson in how to change your perspective because it is not all just about you but now you are required to consider your partner's feelings and emotions. What do you need to set aside for the sake of this relationship? Not that you need to lose yourself, but you need to become your best self – while your partner does the same. You are never required to be a replica of anyone else but always to exemplify what God has created you to be. Being the best version of you will serve your partner as it will give him/her the permission to also be the best version of themselves.

When you have learnt how to do the heavy lifting at this stage in your relationship, it is likely that your relationship will be ready and able to withstand the changes ahead – the changes that are likely to come to challenge the fruit which your relationship will bear.

During this season then develop the patience and grow the muscle as you work hard – it will not always be this way. While you work hard as is required – do not forget to enjoy the process though. It is too early in the game for complaining and whining especially if you are determined to be in here for the long haul. Every season has its pain but there will also be pleasure, seek out both.

It is important too to learn how to communicate with your partner to help him/her to recognize and understand your perspective. This season is about waiting – learning patience and developing the muscle of endurance. It may seem a struggle as you start because you are in the season of no produce – no real evidence that this relationship will bring forth fruit. However, if you wait patiently while being willing to endure through this season, things will change.

What that change will look like depends on what efforts you are willing to put in at this point.

Galatians 6:9 directs us: And let us not be weary in well-doing; for in **due season** we shall reap if we faint not.

You are encouraged therefore to persevere for your due season will come.

Before we move on, be reminded:

- While there is no evidence of fruit at this time, that season will come;

- Perspective is everything and with the right perspective you can enjoy any season;

- Do not lose yourself in the process but bring your best self to the relationship. This gives your partner the permission to do the same; and

- Wait patiently while you build the muscle of endurance.

Bring your best self to your relationship and give your partner the opportunity to do the same

Chapter Two

Your Second Season - Blossoms

There is hope. As this season comes around it brings with it the promise that you are nearer to the outcome which you desire. We watch the tree fill up with blossoms, and there are things which we did not quite expect. Along with the beautiful aroma of the blossoms we now notice that the blossoms fall off the tree so that there is some more cleaning up to do. The smell can be a put off and this new addition attracts flies which can be a nuisance.

Clean-up is still in the plans! You thought you had gotten away from cleaning with the passing of the last season with the fallen leaves. The air filled with the smell of the mango blossom – there is a growing expectation that soon – after a wait which sometimes seems to be too long - you will soon finally be able to consume delicious fruit.

Is this hope enough to get us through the wait? We have come too far - how can we give up now when we are so close? The anticipation rises and our hopes strengthened because with every passing day we know we are closer to our prize. There is still some work as we wait – we still need to clean up to avoid the flies and there are still some leaves. At this stage though we are accustomed to the work. The tasks do not seem as difficult because we have developed some muscle during the last season and we are anticipating the change into the next season. The gratitude we should have for the lessons from before can help us to get through this.

We are beginning to see some evidence which leads us to believe – we can persevere at this point - because we know better is coming. Is it just the blossoms? How far have we come and what do we hope for? Small steps lead to great success if we are willing to stay the course. What may seem to be a struggle is just a point in the journey that teaches us and allows our faith to be strengthened. This lesson is not so hard to go through when we begin to understand that this stage is not the last – the promise is yet to come; but it is coming.

The process is easier to handle because of this promise – light at the end of the tunnel. However, we need to be aware that blossoms may not produce fruit as they may be false, or they may all fall away. Of course, this is very painful after the anticipation that the promise of fruit is now taken away. This could represent the loss of a child, a broken promise to be in for the long haul or death of a spouse.

Remember that this is all part of the seasons of life. The encouragement here is that again this season will change – even despair can turn around and be joy. Hope springs eternal in the human heart and the chance at new life – new relationship – is always possible. This is what the blossom of life holds for each of us – the potential for fruit. Life does not always give us blossoms that we can identify but many things show up to give us hope that not all is lost which should encourage us to constantly hold on to the hope that this season too will change.

With the rains and the blossoms, we notice that there are soon buds which give the promise of the long awaited fruit.

Lesson 2 – Season of promise

When you see the signs of promise our expectation naturally rises. You begin to plan for what lies ahead – a change invigorates you to hope for good things. There is a new energy level as things start to come together, even if we have to wait a little bit longer.

Imagine the possibilities and the promise. New life springs up and the excitement builds. There is a new smell in the air which encourages us to look to the future with expectation that life will get better and brighter.

In this season, the tickle on your sense of smell makes looking at life a bit easier. You can see how even though there is no real evidence of the fruit that it is enough to know that the promise of fruit is real. You can see how things have changed and while there is a long way to maturity, this is the beginning of a new hope where life is worth going the distance because of the promise.

The struggle and the wait seem a little bit more tolerable and the exhaustive toil is easier to face because there is hope. We can put up with the shortcomings and we can see past the insecurities of our partner because there is growth and new life, increased energy which means that we can work it out. It is getting better and time will eventually prove to us that the wait was worth it.

We do not even mind the work now; we can clean up, we can bear with the inconveniences of the shedding of some blossoms and even the flies. No bother now as in our heart we can wait a little bit longer – hopefully not too long --- but a little bit longer as this season will past just like the one before it.

And while we wait for the season to change we can enjoy the whiff of that aroma in the air and the challenges of waiting for the fruit do not now seem unsurmountable. Life is possible because with this change of season we see the growth and potential and become expectant of the fullness of time. What will that time bring to us – maybe abundance, maybe the sweetness of life itself, maybe fresh ideas but who knows because the season will change and will bring its own promise of the unknown and maybe the unexpected.

Can we wait for the change? Is there a lesson to be learnt as we wait? What new challenges will we face during this season that we did not experience in the first season – when we were now coming to our Mango tree. Is there a need to build muscle or is this the season to develop gratitude for the promise and appreciation for the aroma which fills the air? Maybe it is time to grow in patience since we understand that the promise is waiting for us around the corner – in the next breath – we do not want to miss out on what lies ahead of us but alas we have to wait; and as we wait we appreciate and develop patience.

What does this patience teach us? Can we see the promise and be content to learn the lessons of gratitude as we wait it out? Every season, including this one, contains our lessons. May we learn and grow through each season with the resilience and understanding that we are on our way to somewhere and while we journey, we can enjoy whatever life brings to us when we appreciate the lessons along the way.

But what needs to be done? Things have improved and the relationship is on a better footing. You can now see eye to eye and can work on things together and for the sake of the relationship, you are willing to see past certain things. You are in a position to agree that a relationship is good to have.

Relationships require work and relationships are full of promise. In each relationship – parties have to recognize the potential and have to be willing to hold on to the promise that fruit season is ahead – slow and steady - develop patterns which produce the result that is being anticipated.

When both persons acknowledge that there is blossom – promise – be encouraged to know that the best is yet to come. The struggle will be worth it – only if you can hold out until the fruit comes in. Your fruit will be the result of the work you put in – take the time therefore to put in the work.

How important is it to put in the work required? You should be encouraged because it gets easier once you develop the right tools – communication, trust, support of each other, taking the time to understand each other's point of view, allowing each other to grow and become better versions of self, and allow for the variance of opinion. Remember you are individuals travelling through life's journey together – but individuals, nevertheless.

While you should never lose yourself – being part of a team requires submission of self the greater good. You will grow this resilience as you allow yourself the opportunity to go through your seasons together.

Before we move on, be reminded that:

- *The work is still required – but there is light at the end of the tunnel*

- *Adaptability is being built as you implement the lessons from the previous session*

- *Look for the potential – it is there as the season is about to change*

- *This season has its own rewards*

- *While the blossoms may be false, do not despair – still learn the lessons as new seasons are up ahead.*

Chapter Three

Your Third Season – Fruit bearing

Finally, the long-awaited season has arrived!!!!

There is evidence of mangoes on the tree and it is almost as if all the seasons before were well worth going through or even suffering through, to reach to this stage. The fruit bearing season has many rewards for those who enjoy the fruit. The fruit is its own reward and can be used in various ways.

A prudent fruit lover understands that the fruit will not be around forever and may desire to store/freeze some of this fruit for out-of-season enjoyment. Additional ways of use include making of smoothies/drink; use in salads/cakes etc. and can be found to enhance the enjoyment.

Fruit season can represent the full bloom of our aspirations – when after going through the work involved before getting here now the results are evident. This season shows us that there is so much that we have – so much we can do with what we have and so much that we can give. We can even store up some of our effort for later so that in other seasons we are still able to enjoy some of our output. The joy of the blessing is not wasted but we can share who we are with those around.

The rich reward of all the efforts of the other seasons – when we see the first glimpse of the promise and then the gifts on display - is truly the greatest reward. Even though each season has its benefits and its challenges, the reward – in due season – the manifestation of our fruits is reward enough so that we can savor the sweet taste of our fruit.

The fruit comes in many different varieties and size. The flavor depends on which variety it is and when the fruit is harvested and if gathered when the fruit is too young it is not allowed to mature and this will affect its taste. The fruit is available in abundance and some will even fall off the tree for whatever reason. You now recognize that even in the reward stage of waiting on this season to come around, there is work still to be done. The fruit cannot be eaten while on the tree so there is need to pick them. There will be those which have been bitten by monkeys, bats and even picked by the birds. These will need to be separated from those which will be gathered for consumption by family and friends. New muscles are being developed and again you will recognize the value of developing the muscles with the added treat of the enjoyment of the fruit.

The challenge here, as with any seasonal activity, is to recognize that even this season will eventually give way to the next season. The work and the wait serve their purpose and are essential to the ultimate fulfilment of enjoying the reward. Remember that all seasons past but they also come around again and this should help us to bear the challenges/issues of each season with grace – it will past – and it will come around again.

Knowing this, which is a universal law and cannot be influenced by man, should help us to relate to our own relationships. Depending on which season you are in, in your relationship there are aspects of it that are essential to take you through to the next season. Building muscle to deal with the season which is on its way is vital but it should also be important to enjoy/ understand/appreciate the current season – every struggle builds muscle for the struggle which is ahead and when the fulfilment of time comes then in retrospect the joy can be found.

Lesson 3 - Fruit Seasons

The Mango tree and the eventual fruit season is a great reminder that each one of us goes through our seasons and will, through the seasons, grow to the eventual fulfilment of bearing fruit – a full revelation of what has gone into making us that tree.

Note however that not all fruit is created equal. We are all different and it is important for us to understand and appreciate the differences. While on any one tree the fruit will more than likely look and taste the same, there can still be some differences in size and taste, dependent on when the fruit is harvested.

From tree to tree the differences are more evident. The taste, the colour, the size, make up the variety of fruit. Of course, each fruit has its place and is desired by persons for its own value.

Wow – how significant this can be for each of us who believe that we are different and there is nothing wrong with that – variety is the spice of life – and each one can be appreciated for what it is – as it is.

Relationships bring together people with differences. Different is not bad but adds flavor and once this can be appreciated, there is no telling what this variety can add to the spice of life.

It is true of fruit as it is with people. Different does not mean difficult. Different does not mean that we cannot agree to disagree – we can do this without being disagreeable. Each one has their place and their purpose to fulfil. Understanding this makes life beautiful as the flavors can be blended to bring out a new and fantastic result.

How do we enjoy the differences? We need to leave ourselves open to receive so that we can appreciate these differences. Opinions bring new light and perspective which can broaden our own perspective and once open, a new appreciation for the differences in life.

But what happens when the fruit season comes along and there is no fruit? The mango tree will bear fruit in its season. In some fruit seasons there is an abundance but in another fruit-bearing season the evidence is not as compelling. You may need to take a step back and look at what has happened in the other seasons which has led to this outcome.

The condition and nurture of your tree provides the results. Maybe your tree needs some additional dirt, manure or the rains didn't fall in enough quantity to produce the harvest. Could you have watered or use more manure around the tree to ensure the outcome?

The harvest is in direct response to the care given to the tree. Notice that plenty rainfall results in an abundant harvest. Should your tree not produce fruit or not in the quantity which you were hoping for, take a step back and see if you need to pay more attention to the tree.

In life what we give out does come back to us. When we nurture our relationships with love, care and attention we develop a harvest of love care and attention. Will you determine what kind of harvest you desire and work towards it?

It is already a known fact that you cannot get cherries from a mango tree so if you desire mangoes, and you plant that mango tree you will only get mangoes. The quality and quantity of your harvest depends on the investment you make to ensure your harvest.

What if your tree just sits there and complaints or compares itself with other mango trees? This is a tree that has not recognized its purpose. Is it possible that this tree needs to be transplanted because the soil is not good enough? It may very well be the case.

When do you give up on your tree? Have you churned the soil, given it fertilizer, watered and done everything else that you could do and still no result? The season yielded no result, there are no blossoms and consequently no fruit.... cut that tree down...it is good for nothing.

Before we move on, remember that:

- *The intention of life is to grow; if we are not growing then we are stagnating*
- *We are different and it is in being different that makes us (and others) valuable*
- *There is purpose in our journey if we careful to seek out that purpose*
- *You have to make an investment in your relationship*
- *There comes a time to sever ties because the relationship has become toxic and every other effort to make it work has failed.*

Lesson 4 - Abundance

When your mango tree bears as expected, what do you do with your harvest? The fruit season is now here and the fruits of your labour is evident. You know that while there is an abundance of fruit now, this season will not last. What do you do when there is so much fruit, it is too much for you to enjoy all in one go? Can you find creative ways to enjoy, or share, or even store your bounty?

The lesson here is that this long-awaited season has come but it too shall pass. While it is here we can find ways which can lead to an extended enjoyment if we are creative enough.

There is a song which says: *"Memories don't leave like people do, they always stay with you whether they've been good or bad there are something that you have".*

This is so true – but we need to make our memories good.

During the season of an abundance of fruit, a harvest which you have worked hard for and understand that it would not last forever - making memories, good memories ensure that your next season can be enjoyable.

The dry season is coming, what do you have to look forward to - an abundance of good memories. Store up on those memories now in the fruit season - a season of abundance.

Before we move on; remember that:

- *Enjoy the season that you are in*

- *Find creative ways to store up some of this abundance – create lasting memories*

- *Good memories help you get through the tough times.*

Chapter Four

Season Four – Branches: No Leaves

It now looks like our Mango Tree is at the end of its useful life and is destined to be abandoned since it does not look like it can offer anything at all. There are no leaves since the wind has taken all the old, dry leaves and have blown them off the tree. Additionally, there are no blossoms and not one fruit is in sight. Is this really a mango tree, where is the proof? Has this tree stopped being a mango tree because there is no evidence of the fruit?

Indeed not! This is just another season through which this tree must pass until there is another change and the cycle will begin all over again. The truth is that this season is just as necessary as all the other seasons and it is up to us to understand the cycle and appreciate the process on this journey of awaiting your mangoes.

How you wait for the season to change depends on what you expect to be the outcome. Have you been in this season before or is this your first time around? Can you appreciate that the wait for the change to take place and seek to enjoy the process which you wait? Waiting can be a challenge. We think a lot of times, that what we want should happen as soon as we think about it without recognizing that there is as much value in the preparation stage as there is in the fulfilment of the desired outcome.

Maybe your mango tree is at the stage where all the leaves are gone. Remember that it is still a mango tree and as it has produced mangoes previously it will do so again as the season comes around for picking those lovely mangoes.

In the interim, while we wait on our mango tree to move to its next season, we are required to extend due care and attention. We have to recognize that it is due to our care and attention, watering, pruning, adding fertilizer as we tend the roots that our tree will eventually reward us.

Lesson 5 – Be Careful of Hasty Decisions

Waiting is not something that many people like to do. It is however a very necessary process in any journey as we go through the changing seasons. In our relationships we may have come to a point where there is no evidence of any fruit. We had enjoyed the sweets of young love and have experienced the joy of working to build our lives and homes together.

As the years have rolled by maybe it is the pressures of life that have sapped all the fruit out of our relationships and we come to a fork in the road. Our relationship now resembles this mango tree without any evidence of it being a mango tree – no leaves, no blossoms and certainly no fruit.

How we wait for our season to change will determine what happens next. The tree is without evidence of it being a mango tree but remember it is still a mango tree and that will never change. The season for bearing is over and maybe it is time to just hang in there and tend the roots.

Tending to your relationship is vital in ensuring that with the change of each season the relationship stands strong. Our conversations, maintaining respect for each other and our daily interactions go a long way to building a strong relationship. This is how we water, prune and add manure to our tree to ensure that through to the next fruit bearing season there is a guaranteed supply of fruit.

This is not the season to give up, though many persons do, because much effort has already gone into developing this relationship which has produced much good fruit already. Especially if you have gone through every other season before and you are aware of the potential of your tree, you should always be reminded that the season will eventually change.

Before we move on; remember that:

- *How we wait for our season to change will determine what happens next*
- *Sometimes you are called to just hang in there*
- *There is still work to do while you wait – don't grumble*
- *While you wait for the change, don't lose ground*

This is not the season to give up, you have put too much effort into developing this relationship to give up now.

Conclusion - Appreciation of the Seasons

When we come upon a mango tree in its season of dryness, we want to complain and ask why there is no fruit? Again, if we were to come to the mango tree during the season of blossom, we may take the time to appreciate the beautiful scent but may complain that there are more flies attracted to the tree during this time, and also that there is no fruit. During the season of budding, when the rains come and the fruit is evident but not yet ready to be eaten we can look on in anticipation of being able to enjoy the fruit which, again, is not yet ready.

Then the fruit is ripe and ready for the picking and we enjoy the bounty of supply but can still complain about something, and in this case it is the abundance and the work involved in reaping and cleaning.

What is important to note is that each season has its joys and it challenges. When we meet people in their own season it is important for us to recognize and understand that this is just what it is – a season which will change and where, if given time, the joys and challenges can be enjoyed as this relationship bears fruit.

Is there ever a season when you would want to cut down this tree as there is no discernible benefit of having the tree? Maybe there are reasons why this tree may need be hewn down. However, you should carefully consider the circumstances and recognize that if it is just a case for need to change, that whichever season of life the tree is currently in, it will eventually change. Additionally, note that the tree is also a product of its environment and should any adjustments be made to the environment, the tree may very well respond differently. Therefore, careful consideration should be taken of the true benefits of having this tree before any decisions are taken to have the tree destroyed.

Consider that with a little help from an expert gardener or a soil conservation officer, your tree could be saved and go on to produce much fruit, and much reward.

Here's to your long and rewarding relationships.

About The Author (Biography)

Deborah O Lorde of DOL Coaching is a certified Life Coach to individuals who desire more fulfilling relationships. This is achieved through developing interpersonal communication skills to reduce and eliminate frustration and overwhelm at the personal and professional levels.

She works with CEOs and career leaders as well as individuals in her church and community. She has served as an interim Pastor and is a Human Resource Management practitioner where her coaching skills are widely utilized.

www.ingramcontent.com/pod-product-compliance
Lightning Source LLC
LaVergne TN
LVHW021350160826
845679LV00008B/1558

* 9 7 9 8 3 5 7 9 4 2 8 9 0 *